Timeline of mammoth discoveries

5 million years ago

Mammoth species evolve into being. They are roughly the same size as modern African elephants and have long, curved tusks.

1690s

Mammoth remains, including tusks, begin to be displayed in Europe. This is when the word 'mammoth' first comes into use.

4,500 years ago

Mammoths become extinct. Scientists are uncertain whether this was due to the advent of a warmer climate or overhunting by humans.

1796

The French naturalist and zoologist Georges Cuvier is the first to identify mammoths as an extinct species of elephant.

1799

The first complete woolly mammoth skeleton is found in Siberia by Russian botanist Mikhail Adams, and it becomes known as the Adams Mammoth.

May 2007

Lyuba, a mummified female woolly mammoth calf, is discovered by a reindeer breeder in Russia's Arctic Yamal Peninsula. She is the best preserved mammoth ever found.

December 2005

British, American and German scientists manage to assemble a complete mammoth DNA strand.

2015

There are currently several major scientific projects underway to bring mammoths back from extinction, either through cloning or artificial insemination. However, technology has not yet advanced enough to make this possible.

Mammoth migration map

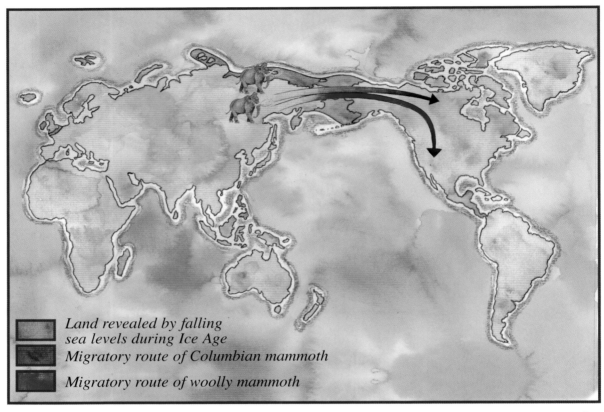

Land revealed by falling sea levels during Ice Age

Migratory route of Columbian mammoth

Migratory route of woolly mammoth

Woolly and Columbian mammoths migrated from Asia to North America via the Bering land bridge, which linked Russia and Alaska. During ice ages, the sea levels are lower and land that is normally underwater becomes accessible for a while. This means that mammoths and other species from Asia and Africa were able to cross the Bering land bridge when it emerged from the sea as glaciers formed and water levels fell.

The Columbian mammoth arrived in North America around 1.8 million years ago, settling across the territory that is now the USA and travelling as far south as parts of Mexico. The woolly mammoth followed 100,000 years ago, but it remained in the north in Alaska and Canada instead.

Author:
John Malam studied ancient history and archaeology at the University of Birmingham, after which he worked as an archaeologist at the Ironbridge Gorge Museum in Shropshire, England. He is now an author, specialising in nonfiction books for children. He lives in Cheshire, England, with his wife and two children.

Artist:
David Antram was born in Brighton, England, in 1958. He studied at Eastbourne College of Art and then worked in advertising for fifteen years before becoming a full-time artist. He has illustrated many children's nonfiction books.

Series Creator:
David Salariya was born in Dundee, Scotland. He has illustrated a wide range of books and has created and designed many new series for publishers both in the U.K. and overseas. In 1989, he established The Salariya Book Company. He lives in Brighton with his wife, illustrator Shirley Willis, and their son Jonathan.

Editor:
Karen Barker Smith

Assistant Editor:
Michael Ford

Published in Great Britain in MMXVI by
Book House, an imprint of
The Salariya Book Company Ltd
25 Marlborough Place, Brighton BN1 1UB
www.salariya.com
www.book-house.co.uk
ISBN: 978-1-910706-46-6

SALARIYA

1 3 5 7 9 8 6 4 2

A CIP catalogue record for this book is available from the British Library.

Printed and bound in China.

Visit our website at **www.book-house.co.uk**
or go to **www.salariya.com** for **free** electronic versions of:
You Wouldn't Want to be an Egyptian Mummy!
You Wouldn't Want to be a Roman Gladiator!
You Wouldn't Want to be a Polar Explorer!
You Wouldn't Want to sail on a 19th-Century Whaling Ship!

PAPER FROM
SUSTAINABLE
FORESTS

You Wouldn't Want to Be a™
Mammoth Hunter!

I can make sixteen arrowheads from this block of flint.

Chip Chip Chip

Written by
John Malam

Illustrated by
David Antram

Created and designed by
David Salariya

Dangerous Beasts You'd Rather Not Encounter

BOOK HOUSE

Contents

Introduction

Long, long ago, large areas of Europe, Asia and North America were covered in ice and snow. The temperature was much lower than it is today. In this permanently cold environment, the ice cap from the North Pole spread southwards. Today's countries of Canada, northern United States, Greenland, Iceland, the British Isles, Denmark, Norway, Sweden, Finland, and parts of Russia and Poland were all buried beneath a layer of ice up to 2 km (1 mile) thick.

This is the Ice Age – the world of 15,000 years ago. Welcome to life at the edge of this frozen world. You are a hunter following the trail of mammoths as they cross a vast, treeless wilderness. You camp where your people have always sheltered. You leave your mark on the walls of caves. You fight your enemies. You kill mammoths. Life is hard and can be short. If you are brave and strong, you will be successful. If you are not, then you wouldn't want to be an Ice Age mammoth hunter!

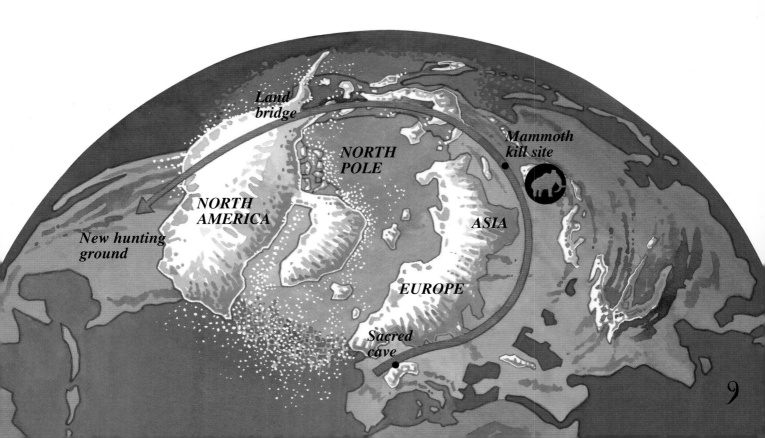

Land bridge

NORTH POLE

Mammoth kill site

NORTH AMERICA

ASIA

New hunting ground

EUROPE

Sacred cave

It's cold! Living in the Ice Age

Animals of the Ice Age:

ON THE MENU. Learn to recognise the animals around you. Know the edible ones, such as aurochs and mammoth, and the ones that will eat you, like the cave lion and cave bear.

You live in a small group of hunter-gatherers. You were born into this close-knit group. Your people have taught you everything you know and, when the time comes, you will pass your knowledge on to your descendants – if you live that long. Your group is preparing to go on a hunting trip. Sharp tools are being made from pieces of flint, and animal skins are being scraped clean and then stitched together to make clothes.

Woolly mammoth (edible)

Aurochs (edible)

Cave lion (avoid)

Bison (edible)

Woolly rhinoceros (avoid)

Cave bear (avoid)

Reindeer (edible)

Wild horse (edible)

Cave hyena (nuisance)

10

You share the land with many species of large mammals. They have adapted to life in the cold by growing woolly coats to keep them warm. Humans make fire to keep out the cold. They also use it to cook their food.

Handy hint

Keep warm. Learn the secret of making fire by twisting a stick on a piece of wood quickly. The friction will light a fire.

Antler needles are best for sewing mammoth hide.

Whack!

11

Darkness! A visit to a sacred cave

You walk east until you reach a cave that goes deep into the ground. It's a sacred place for your people and has been visited by groups of hunters for thousands of years. As you enter the mysterious darkness, you feel like you are travelling into another world. Here you can make contact with spirits and summon the magical powers to help you in the hunt. Those who have been here before have left their marks on the cave walls and ceiling. Images of animals, some painted, some scratched, some sculpted from clay, are all around. Some show animals with spears in them. If you want success in the hunt, you must also make an image of the animal you hope to kill.

A cave artist's tools:

Blowpipes

Stone points or gravers

Ochre

Brushes

Oil lamp

Oil lamps burn brightly in the darkness, giving you light to see by. Crush some ochre, a natural pigment, and mix it with oil to make red, brown and yellow paint. Or use lumps of it like crayons, drawing straight onto the rock. Make brushes from animal hair, the chewed ends of sticks, or just dip your fingers into the paint. Use stone points to scratch pictures, and clay to make sculptures.

Handy hint

Put your hand against the wall, then spit paint through your blowpipe all over it. Your hand image will live with the spirits, always there to guide you.

This place is so spooky!

FINGER PAINTING. Paint long, broad lines with your fingers, or use your fingertips to make dots of colour.

CLAY. Use soft clay to make life-size animal sculptures. Model them straight onto the cave walls.

13

Magic! The mammoth hunters' dance

The magic man

One of your group is a shaman, or a holy man, who has great powers. Before the hunt begins he will lead you in a magical dance. You will chant strange words and noises, and sing and shout to make contact with the spirits of the animals you wish to hunt. The spirits will hear you, and the animals will know you are coming for them. As you dance, your ears will be filled with sound, such as steady beats from drums, shrill notes from a flute, and the whirring of a roarer as it spins and twists through the air. You will dance until you are in a wild, trance-like state of mind. Then you will be truly ready for the hunt.

ANTLER HEADDRESS. The shaman wears an animal skin and antler headdress so he feels close to the animal spirits.

ROARER. A roarer is an oval piece of bone, ivory, or wood attached to a length of thread. As it spins through the air it hums. The faster it twists, the louder it gets until it roars.

Roarer

Skin drum

Bone flute

Weapons!
A mammoth hunter's toolkit

If you stand any chance of killing a mammoth, you'll need powerful weapons. Luckily for you, nature has provided all the raw materials a hunter needs to make weapons. All you've got to do is find the flint, bone, wood, leather, feathers and resin, then turn them into bows, arrows, spears, clubs, axes, knives, slings and points. Learn how to use your weapons once you've gathered them together. When the time comes, you'll be able to make every one of them find its target and, hopefully, kill a mammoth.

Spear-thrower

Boomerang

Sling

SPEAR-THROWERS.
Choose a long, straight wooden pole for your spear. Carve the tip into a sharp point. Launch your spear from a bone spear-thrower – it will make your spear fly further.

BOOMERANG AND SLING.
Make your boomerang from wood. It will come back to you after flying in a curve. A strip of leather will make a sling. You will use it to throw pebbles.

These arrows can even pierce mammoth hide.

Boo!

Handy hint

Give your wooden spear a hard tip by heating it over a fire to dry its sap. Make sure it doesn't catch fire!

BONE AND STONE POINTS. Make barbed harpoon points from antler or bone, and chip flint into lethal points. Stick them to your weapons with resin, or bind them with thread.

BOW AND ARROWS. Make your bow from yew wood, the bowstring from animal gut, the arrowheads from flint, and use feathers for arrow flights.

FLINT TOOLS. Take a lump of flint and roughly shape it. Use a piece of antler to break off tiny flakes to make a razor-sharp edge.

17

Shelter! Mammoth bone houses

our journey has taken you across a large field of grassy vegetation. This is a good sign, since mammoths eat these plants. You're sure it won't be long before you see a herd and move in for the kill. Practise your hunting skills on other animals that live nearby, such as bison and aurochs. They can provide food for many days. With no caves in the area, you'll have to make shelters from whatever you can find lying around. Make tents from branches covered with skins or grass. The best houses are made from old mammoth bones and tusks.

Making leather clothes:

2. CLEAN THE HIDE

1. SKIN AN ANIMAL

I want one like they've got!

3. DRY THE HIDE

4. CUT THE LEATHER

5. MAKE HOLES IN THE LEATHER

6. SEW THE PIECES

Handy hint

Make the entrance to your bone house from a curved pair of mammoth tusks. Hang a flap of leather over the tusks to act as a door.

It's dry as a bone in there.

We've got a modern home.

At last! You see mammoths

The mammoth family:

The grassy landscape is mammoth country. Look for signs that tell you these great, hairy beasts are nearby, such as chewed branches stripped of bark, holes in the ground where roots have been pulled up, and areas of trampled and nibbled grass. Most of all, you should be looking for piles of fresh mammoth

MAMMUTHUS MERIDIONALIS
(the ancestor of all mammoths)

MAMMUTHUS TROGONTHERII
(the steppe mammoth)

MAMMUTHUS PRIMIGENIUS
(the woolly mammoth)

MAMMUTHUS COLUMBI
(the American mammoth)

Why is the grass moving?

dung! As you follow the signs, crouch low or crawl on your belly. Be as quiet as you can and do not make any sudden movements. When you see the mammoths, look for an old or a weak animal separated from the herd. This one will be easier and safer to attack than a mammoth that is fit and strong.

Handy hint

Track the mammoths by following their dung trail. They drop lots of dung balls, each about 20 cm across – about the size of your head!

What a mammoth eats:

VEGETARIAN FOOD. Mammoths eat grass, low-growing plants, roots, bark and leaves. They use the tip of their trunk like a finger and thumb to pinch and pull at plants.

Grass

Roots

Bark

Leaves

That one doesn't look like it's in very good shape.

Kill! You catch a mammoth

Dig a big pit and cover the top with branches and grass. Circle the old or weak mammoth, then move towards it. When you are within spear-throwing distance, if the mammoth has not already seen, heard, or smelled you, stand up and shout, throw stones and prod it with your spear. When the mammoth reaches the trap, it will crash to the bottom of the pit. Now you must kill it. Drive your spear deep into it, piercing its vital organs. But watch out for its tusks – even an old mammoth can put up a good fight.

Mammoth traps:

WAYS TO TRAP A MAMMOTH. Lure it into a pit; force it over a cliff; drop a log on it to break its neck; drive it into a pool of sticky tar; or chase it onto thin ice.

Pit fall

Cliff fall

Falling log

Tar pit

Thin ice

22

23

Danger! Attacked by rivals

You might think now that you've killed a mammoth, you can enjoy a meaty feast. Think again! Your dead mammoth means a free lunch to scavenging animals – and not just the four-legged type. While you've faced the dangers, you've been watched by another group of hunters.

Now they're here to steal your food. They hope that the struggle to kill the mammoth has left you weak and out of weapons. For your sake, you hope you have enough strength to defeat your enemy. The short and violent fight leaves injured men on both sides. Some injuries will heal, others won't. One of the members in your group has been hit with an arrow.

Ouch! They got me!

Possible injuries:

CUTS AND BRUISES. Leaves and grass will help stop the bleeding and swelling.

BITES AND PRODS. You might be crushed under a hoof, stabbed by a pointed tusk, or bitten.

Handy hint

Shout and scream at the attackers. Scare them with your battle cries. Make scary faces.

ARROW AND SPEAR WOUNDS. Be brave as someone pulls the arrow out.

BROKEN BONES. A broken limb is serious. It will need sticks tied to it to keep it still until the bone heals.

It'll be our dinner soon.

Buried! Disposing of the dead

Your friend has died. His wound was too serious; there was nothing you could do for him. However, now that he is dead, you can help his spirit as it travels into the next world. First, find a place to bury his body. A cave is best, since you believe it is an entrance to the spirit world. Then dig a shallow grave. Lay the body on its side and cover it with red ochre. Surround it with food and all the things that he will need in the next life. Finally, as the body is covered with stones, say your goodbyes. You hope that when your time is up, you too will be given a warrior's burial.

Grave goods:

BEADS (right). Bury him with his necklace made from shells, teeth and pierced stones.

OCHRE (below). This is the same stuff you use to make paint. Sprinkle it over the body.

FOOD (below). Place a chunk of meat in the grave.

TOOLS (below). Put a flint axe and scraper in his grave, for use in the next life.

WEAPONS (below). Bury the man's spear with him.

Necklace

Ochre

Food

Tools

Feast! Mammoth for dinner

Nothing goes to waste. At the kill site, everyone helps carve up the mammoth's body. Flint knives slice through the thick hide. Flesh is cut from bone and roasted over open fires. Tusks are yanked from their sockets for their fine ivory – it will be carved into beautiful objects. The hide is scraped clean to make clothes and shoes of tough leather. Small bones are sharpened into needles and points. Big bones are prized for the marrow inside them.

Carving mammoth ivory and bone:

ANIMAL FIGURES. Shape a bone into a model of a horse or a bison.

ART OBJECTS. Decorate squares of bone with patterns of lines and dots.

Wait until it's cooked, greedy.

Slurp Slurp

BEADS AND BRACELETS. Make ivory bracelets from slices of tusk and beads from bones and teeth.

'VENUS' FIGURINES. Make statues of women from ivory.

HUMAN FIGURES. Carefully carve out the head and face of a person and polish it until it's smooth.

Handy hint

Don't waste good food! Split open the mammoth's big bones to get at the tasty, fatty marrow inside.

We'll smoke this to feed us through the winter.

Long march!
Crossing the land bridge

After you've had your fill, it's time to begin your travels once again. As a hunter-gatherer you never stay in one place for very long. It's your nature to live as a nomad, following your prey wherever it goes, gathering plants along the way. But where did the mammoth herd go? As you pick up the trail, you continue walking east and cross a frozen wilderness. You have never seen anywhere like this before. Perhaps you and your group are the first humans to ever set foot here. You see huge blocks of ice floating on the sea and strange creatures swimming in the freezing water. You hope that the mammoth trail leads to a warmer place, taking you away from this icy land to somewhere new.

What ugly creatures!

Bridge between continents:

BERINGIA. This is the name given to the land bridge that joined Asia to North America during the last ice age.

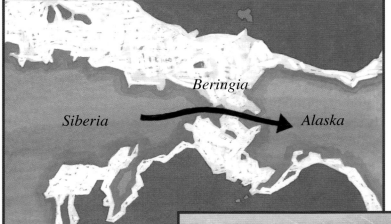

Siberia · *Beringia* · *Alaska*

Handy hint

Scratch signs on a rock. They will show people who come after you which way to travel and lead them to the herds of mammoth.

MIGRATION. Animals crossed the land bridge from one continent to the other. When humans first used it about 15,000 years ago, the peopling of the Americas began.

RISING SEA LEVEL. When the glaciers retreat the ice age will end. The sea level and the land bridge will be flooded. From then on the continents will be separated by a sea channel.

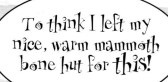

To think I left my nice, warm mammoth bone hut for **this!**

You reach a new world

You leave the icy wasteland behind and move steadily southwards. Generations of ice age hunters will make the same crossing between the continents. Slowly they will spread out to colonise the new world, which will one day be America. Mammoths live here – taller than the ones in Europe and Asia, but not as hairy. Life carries on for your people, tracking, killing and eating your prey. As time passes, the land bridge is forgotten and it slowly sinks beneath the sea. Something else disappears, too – the mammoths. Your descendants will hunt these creatures until they become extinct.

There don't seem to be many of these left.

What happened next?

CLOVIS POINTS. Hunters in North America started making a new type of stone point. We call them 'Clovis' points, after a place in New Mexico where they were found. This one (right) is actual size.

OVERKILL. People who used Clovis points were hunters who killed large mammals. Some experts say that by 11,000 years ago they had killed all the mammoths in North America.

ROAR

Handy hint

If mammoth meat is hard to find, switch to a new diet — a mixture of plants and meat.

CHANGING HABITAT. Another theory is that mammoths died out because rising sea temperatures caused trees to spread, destroying their natural habitat.

LAST OF THE MAMMOTHS. Mammoths survived until 4,000 years ago. The last ones lived on Wrangel Island, in the Arctic Ocean. They were dwarf mammoths, only 2 metres (7 feet) tall.

DEEP FREEZE. Some mammoths that died of natural causes became frozen in ice. Their mummified bodies have been dug up and put on display.

Glossary

Aurochs Wild cattle that once lived in Europe and are now extinct.

Beringia The name given to the land bridge that once joined Asia to North America.

Boomerang A stick that when thrown will fly back to the thrower.

Clovis The name given to prehistoric people who were among the first to live in North America.

Extinction When a species of animal completely dies out.

Flint A type of stone that can be shaped to make tools.

Friction Heat generated by rubbing two things together.

Harpoon A spear-like weapon with a rope attached, used to catch sea creatures.

Hunter-gatherer A person who hunts and gathers food in the wild, moving from one campsite to the next.

Ice age The time when the world's temperature was lower and ice covered large areas of land.

Ice cap A permanent covering of ice and snow at the North and South Poles.

Ivory A whitish material that mammoth and elephant tusks are made of.

Land bridge A place where areas of land are joined, allowing animals to cross between them.

Mammoth An extinct member of the elephant family. The word may come from two Estonian words – *maa* (earth) and *mutt* (mole).

Marrow A soft, fatty substance that is found inside bones.

Nomad A person who wanders from place to place.

Ochre A yellow, red, or brown mineral used as a colouring in paint.

Point A piece of stone or bone shaped into a pointed tool.

Resin A sticky substance that mainly oozes from fir and pine trees.

Roarer A type of musical instrument, sometimes called a bull roarer. It makes a whirring noise.

Shaman A person believed to have the power to make contact with the spirit world.

Spear-thrower A bone or wooden tool used to launch a spear and throw it a great distance. Also called an atlatl.

Steppe An open grassy plain with few trees.

'Venus' figure A carved figure of a woman, often made with exaggerated bodily features. Made in Europe in the ice age. Their purpose is unclear.

35

Index

Cave paintings

The roots of writing go as far back as the cave dwellers who lived many thousands of years ago. What made these early people begin writing, and how did they go about it? The earliest writing was probably meant to tell others about where to find food or shelter. Some simple marks made with basic tools could get that message across.

Paintings on cave walls, lit by flickering flames, told stories of battles and hunting, and showed how people could protect themselves against animals, the weather and other people! Mammoth hunters like the ones in this book would have drawn pictures of the animals they killed and the dangers they faced every day.

Some of the most famous, vibrant and detailed paintings can be found in the Lascaux cave complex in southwestern France. The cave contains nearly 2,000 animal, human and abstract figures, which are estimated to be more than 17,000 years old.

37

Other extinct species

Andrewsarchus In 1923, an ancient skull more than 1 m (3 ft) in length and with huge teeth was discovered in Mongolia. It belonged to an extinct animal that lived 35 million years ago, probably the largest meat-eating mammal ever. This gigantic creature, named Andrewsarchus, lived much like today's hyenas, scavenging for food, chasing away predators and stealing their kill.

Dodo Dodos were giant, flightless pigeons that lived on the island of Mauritius in the Indian Ocean. They had no predators until Europeans arrived on the island in the fifteenth century, introducing pigs, dogs, rats, and cats that found the birds and their eggs easy prey. The dodo also provided easy food for passing sailors. By the seventeenth century, the dodo was extinct.

Giant deer Two million years ago, the giant deer, or Irish elk, roamed vast woodlands stretching from China to Ireland. The stags had huge antlers up to 4 m (13 ft) across. Fossilised antlers reveal marks where the stags locked them together in combat – just as they do today.

Phorusrhacos and Gastornis

These huge birds had tiny wings and could not fly. They were meat-eating hunters that stalked forests and swamps, looking for mammals to ambush and eat. Gastornis lived around 50 million years ago in Europe and North America. Phorusrhacos lived in South America about half a million years ago.

Ambulocetus was one of the first sea mammals. It was an ancestor of the whale, but it didn't look anything like the whales we know today. It lived in Asia, and could walk on land and swim in the sea. A meat-eating predator the size of a big sea lion, it lay in wait to ambush passing prey. It became extinct 50 million years ago.